W9-BKL-989

A PJ LIBRARY FAMILY GUIDE FOR STARTING THE JEWISH NEW YEAR

A TIME TO GROW

Ready to start a new Jewish year? Let's go!

A TIME TO GROW

Happy New Year, or in Hebrew, *Shanah tovah*!

The three-week Jewish holiday season that begins with **Rosh Hashanah** (Jewish New Year) is a celebration of growth.

On the High Holidays of Rosh Hashanah (also called the "birthday of the world") and **Yom Kippur** (Day of Forgiving), we look back on the past year and take responsibility for our actions. We think about ways to make ourselves and our world better. We reconnect with family and friends and look ahead with hope to a sweet new year.

On the harvest festival of **Sukkot** (Festival of Small Huts), we tune into growth in the natural world — crops that sustain us, rain that nourishes the earth, and the sight and scent of bountiful plants that bring us joy. And finally, on **Simchat Torah** (Rejoicing with the Torah), we complete the annual reading of the Torah (the first five books of the Bible) and begin it all over again — a cycle of reading and storytelling that never grows old, because each year we are growing right along with these stories.

This is the journey that Jewish tradition invites us to take each new year as our families continue to grow. Let's celebrate together!

WHAT'S IN THIS GUIDE?

This guide offers ways for families to celebrate the new Jewish year at home. Because each family is unique, the guide is designed so you can choose those parts that meet the needs and interests of your family. Each section is devoted to a different holiday, presenting tips on preparing for the holiday and ideas for celebrating as a family.

What's in the Picture?
A simple visual introduction to Rosh Hashanah, Yom Kippur, and Sukkot

Step-by-Step Rituals for Family Meals
Blessings, symbols, and explanations to make holiday meals festive

Hands-On Activities and Recipes
24 different family projects to add fun and meaning to these holidays

Conversation Starters
Prompts for discussions about how we can grow as individuals, families, and communities

Unpacking High Holiday Prayers
Family-friendly insights into five Rosh Hashanah and Yom Kippur prayers

PLAN AHEAD

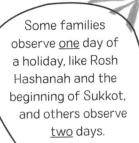

Some families observe <u>one</u> day of a holiday, like Rosh Hashanah and the beginning of Sukkot, and others observe <u>two</u> days. Learn more at **pjlibrary.org/ calendar**.

FOOD SHOPPING: Symbolic foods are eaten on Rosh Hashanah. See pages 19 and 21-23 before you head to the grocery store.

SUKKAH: If you are planning to build a *sukkah* (temporary hut) for Sukkot or to purchase a ritual *lulav* and *etrog* for shaking, visit **pjlibrary.org/sukkot** for ordering and building tips.

CONTENTS FOR

ROSH HASHANAH

GETTING READY

Sweet Greetings 8

Have a Blast! 10

Challah in the Round 11

What's in the Picture? — Preparing the Evening Meal 13

Finishing Touches 15

ROSH HASHANAH EVENING

Holiday Blessings 16

Symbolic New Year Foods 21

ROSH HASHANAH DAY

What's All the Praying About? 24

Tashlich (Casting Away Our Mistakes) 32

Family finger foods
Pages 21–23

THE TEN DAYS OF RETURNING 35

YOM KIPPUR

GETTING READY

What's in the Picture? — A Different Day 40

Final Preparation 43

YOM KIPPUR EVENING

How We Open Yom Kippur 44

YOM KIPPUR DAY

Covering Over & Planting New 45

The Story of Jonah 47

Goals & Challenges for the New Year 48

CONCLUSION OF YOM KIPPUR

Closing the Gates & Ending the Fast 50

Unpacking Rosh Hashanah and Yom Kippur prayers
Pages 24–31

THIS GUIDE

SUKKOT

GETTING READY

What's in the Picture? — A Hut of One's Own   52

Stew Under the Stars   57

Close-Up: Lulav & Etrog   58

SUKKOT EVENING

Holiday Blessings   60

Family Activities   64

Shaking
the lulav
Page 63

SIMCHAT TORAH

Finishing
and
restarting
the Torah
Page 72

GETTING READY

Appreciating Rain   68

Candy-Apple Making   69

Crafting a Torah   70

SIMCHAT TORAH EVENING

Dancing with the Torah   71

SIMCHAT TORAH DAY

Never-Ending Story   72

EPILOGUE: ON FARMING & GARDENING   74

Worksheet:
Family
Conversations
Pages 77-80

ROSH HASHANAH

The Jewish calendar is based on the cycle of the moon, which grows into a full moon and then disappears about every 30 days. The Jewish New Year begins with the transition from the Hebrew month named *Elul* to the Hebrew month of *Tishrei* (typically sometime in September or early October).

In Jewish tradition, people gather during Elul in the predawn darkness to sing *Selichot* (Hebrew for "special poems of forgiveness"). Then Rosh Hashanah begins on the first of Tishrei, when a small sliver of the new moon appears in the evening sky.

The Jewish New Year is called **Rosh Hashanah** (ROHSH hah-shah-NAH) — *rosh* is "head" and *hashanah* is "the year." In Hebrew the word "year" (*shanah*) comes from a root meaning "to change."

Each new year is an opportunity for change and growth. How will the world change this year? How will <u>you</u> change this year?

GETTING READY

SWEET GREETINGS

How do we greet one another on the Jewish New Year? We call out "*Shanah tovah!*" (shah-NAH toh-VAH) — Have a good year! — or "*Shanah tovah u'metukah!*" (shah-NAH toh-VAH oo-meh-too-KAH) — Have a good and sweet year!

A key Rosh Hashanah custom for making things sweet is dipping apples in honey (see **Symbolic New Year Foods** on page 21).

Shanah tovah u'metukah!

8

MAKE APPLE DESSERT & CARDS

With a supply of apples — store-bought or handpicked — you can try these activities.

MAKE APPLE CARDS

Many people send cards to their friends and families around Rosh Hashanah to wish them a happy new year. You can create apple stamps to make your own homemade cards.

SUPPLIES

APPLES	PAPER PLATES
FORKS	HEAVY CARD STOCK
ACRYLIC PAINT	FINE-TIPPED MARKER

1. Cut the apples in half. Any shape works, but if you cut them across the middle horizontally, you'll find a star.

2. Stick a fork in the back of the apple for a handle.

3. Spread paint out on a paper plate. Dip the apple in the paint, then stamp it on your card stock.

4. Let paint dry, then, using a marker, embellish with a little stem or leaf. Add a New Year's message such as "*Shanah tovah* — Happy New Year!"

EASY BAKED APPLE DESSERT

Make your family a sweet treat for a sweet new year.

INGREDIENTS

4 APPLES

3 TBSP MELTED BUTTER

2 TBSP HONEY (PLUS MORE FOR DRIZZLING)

1/2 CUP ROLLED OATS

1/2 CUP RAISINS

Preheat oven to 375 degrees. Carefully core the apples with a paring knife (a grown-up's job). Mix 2 tablespoons of the butter and the honey, oats, and raisins together in a small bowl, then scoop the mixture into the cored apples. Brush apples with the remaining tablespoon of butter. Arrange apples in a baking dish or on a cookie sheet and bake for 20 to 25 minutes or until apple pierces easily with a sharp knife. Cool for a few minutes, drizzle with a little more honey, and enjoy!

HAVE A BLAST!

Hear the shofar and make your own

In the Bible, Rosh Hashanah is not called Rosh Hashanah. It's called *Yom Teruah*, the day of blasting the *shofar* (ram's horn).

On Rosh Hashanah, the voice of the shofar is like a wake-up call: Pay attention to yourself and ways you can improve! Pay attention to the world and how you can help make it better!

The shofar is sounded 100 times during a traditional Rosh Hashanah service. And a long and loud shofar blast marks the end of Yom Kippur.

While the blower must first take a big breath, the shofar only sounds when the air blows out. This is a symbol for Rosh Hashanah: we turn inward to fix ourselves so we can then burst out and contribute to the world.

Here are the four shofar sounds we blow on Rosh Hashanah and Yom Kippur:

1 **TEKIAH** (THE SINGLE BLOW)

2 **SHEVARIM** (THREE "BROKEN" BLOWS)

3 **TRUAH** (NINE OR MORE RAPID BLOWS)

4 **TEKIAH GEDOLAH** (THE GREAT BLAST)

HANDS ON!

MAKE YOUR OWN SHOFAR

A real shofar is made from a ram's horn, and it takes some skill to blow it. You can make a pretend shofar at home that's easy to "blow," since the sound is your own voice.

SUPPLIES

LARGE PAPER PLATE

STAPLER

MASKING TAPE

1 **Roll the paper plate** into a cone and staple it in place. (You may need an adult's help with this.)

2 **Bend the paper plate** to look like a horn. Use masking tape to help hold the shape. Then wrap the whole shofar in masking tape to give it a horn-like look.

3 **Hold the shofar up** to your mouth and make loud shofar noises, letting everyone around you know it's time to pay attention and make the world better!

Visit pjlibrary.org/grow to hear the shofar sounds.

CHALLAH IN THE ROUND

Bake In the New Year

Rosh Hashanah is called the "birthday of the world." Celebrating the creation of the world is a time when we can re-create our own lives — remembering mistakes we made last year and turning things around for next year.

Or in the words of PJ Library author Linda Heller: "When each of us is the **best we can be**, then the world is the best place that **it** can be." (And that's a real birthday present to the world!)

On Rosh Hashanah a symbol of making ourselves and the world more whole is eating a round challah. A circle has no beginning or end, so a round challah expresses our hope for a year of infinite — lots and lots of! — blessings.

INGREDIENTS

To make two round challah loaves, you'll need:

1½ TBSP YEAST
2½ CUPS WARM WATER
1 TSP PLUS ½ CUP SUGAR
½ CUP VEGETABLE OIL
1 TBSP SALT
8 CUPS FLOUR
1 CUP RAISINS (OPTIONAL)

DIRECTIONS

Dissolve the yeast in the water with 1 teaspoon of sugar. Whisk the mixture together, then add the oil, salt, and remaining sugar. Add the flour gradually, mixing well and then working it in with your hands. Take turns kneading as a family for about 10-15 minutes, until the dough is smooth and elastic. Work in the raisins (optional). Cover the bowl with a towel and leave it in the refrigerator overnight. The next morning, let the dough warm to room temperature, then punch it down and separate into two portions.

Turn to the next page for braiding.

BRAID A ROUND CHALLAH

Challah is usually shaped in a simple long braid, but you can turn any challah recipe into a Rosh Hashanah recipe by braiding it in the round.

1 When you reach the braiding stage, shape the dough into six strands of equal length.

---

2 Lay three strands horizontally on a floured surface, then weave the other three strands into them vertically. Lift the bottom strands as needed to weave the top strands in. The ends of the strands will stick out.

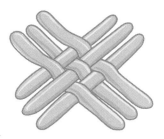

3 Now braid the ends together on all four sides. Gently tuck the braided edges underneath the middle section. Repeat steps 1 through 3 to create your second loaf.

Grease two round baking tins and transfer your loaves into them. Let the dough rise for another hour, then bake at 350 degrees for 20–25 minutes or until golden brown. If desired, glaze with a mixture of warm honey and a drop of water.

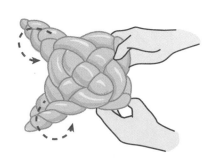

WHAT'S IN THE PICTURE?

PREPARING THE EVENING MEAL

Take a few minutes to look at this scene. Turn the page for explanations.

What special things do you see at this Rosh Hashanah meal?

The Rosh Hashanah evening meal features traditional foods and blessings. The custom of a special Rosh Hashanah meal goes back more than 1,500 years to a Jewish book of commentary and laws called the Talmud, which describes certain foods to eat on Rosh Hashanah.

Over time, blessings were added to these foods to help inspire people to act better in the new year. The tradition grew over time to include more symbolic foods, and various dishes became popular in different Jewish communities around the world.

Good news for kids! The Rosh Hashanah meal highlights sweet foods, symbolizing our desire to have a sweet new year.

WHAT'S IN THE PICTURE?

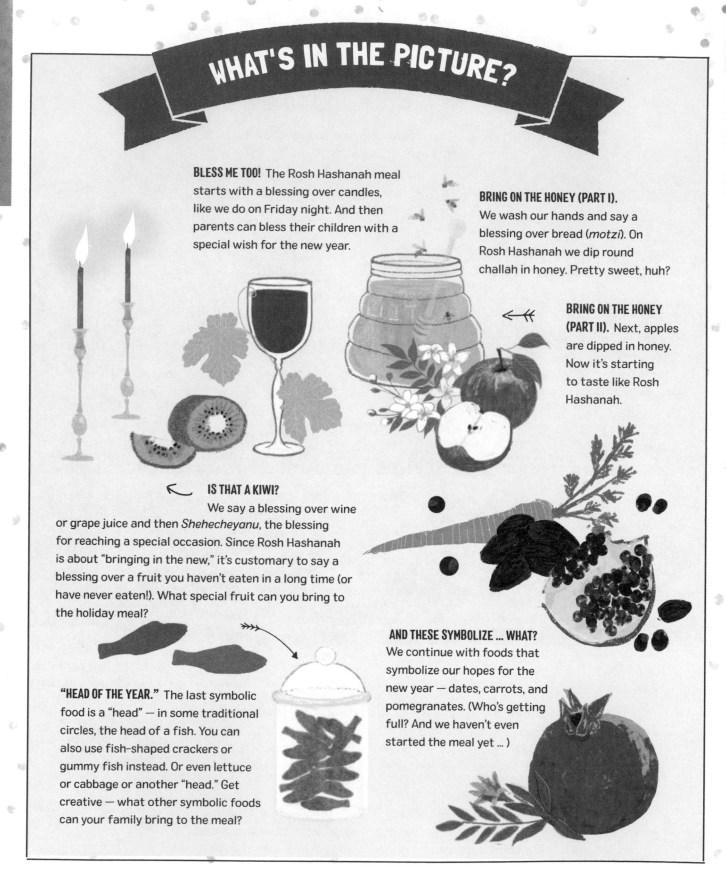

BLESS ME TOO! The Rosh Hashanah meal starts with a blessing over candles, like we do on Friday night. And then parents can bless their children with a special wish for the new year.

BRING ON THE HONEY (PART I). We wash our hands and say a blessing over bread (*motzi*). On Rosh Hashanah we dip round challah in honey. Pretty sweet, huh?

BRING ON THE HONEY (PART II). Next, apples are dipped in honey. Now it's starting to taste like Rosh Hashanah.

IS THAT A KIWI? We say a blessing over wine or grape juice and then *Shehecheyanu*, the blessing for reaching a special occasion. Since Rosh Hashanah is about "bringing in the new," it's customary to say a blessing over a fruit you haven't eaten in a long time (or have never eaten!). What special fruit can you bring to the holiday meal?

AND THESE SYMBOLIZE ... WHAT? We continue with foods that symbolize our hopes for the new year — dates, carrots, and pomegranates. (Who's getting full? And we haven't even started the meal yet ...)

"HEAD OF THE YEAR." The last symbolic food is a "head" — in some traditional circles, the head of a fish. You can also use fish-shaped crackers or gummy fish instead. Or even lettuce or cabbage or another "head." Get creative — what other symbolic foods can your family bring to the meal?

FINISHING TOUCHES

Two more ways to liven up your holiday meal

POP OPEN A POMEGRANATE

Pomegranates go way back in Jewish history — they're one of the seven native species of ancient Israel and are a traditional food at Rosh Hashanah. Some people think that the apple in the Garden of Eden was actually a pomegranate! Pomegranate seeds are delicious, but getting at them can be tricky. Try this technique:

Cut the fruit in half vertically from stem end to flower end (a grown-up's job). Then cut each half in two again.

 **Place the pomegranate halves in a big bowl of water.** Dig your fingers into the fruit to separate the seeds (called arils) from the white fleshy parts (albedo). The seeds will sink to the bottom of the bowl. You can remove the floating parts, then drain the bowl. You'll be left with a generous pile of glistening red seeds.

Enjoy!

MAKE PERSONALIZED PLACE CARDS

Want to make Rosh Hashanah dinner feel even more festive? Make a place card for each person with a special surprise inside.

SUPPLIES

INDEX CARDS

MARKERS

STICKERS

1. Fold index cards in half. On the outside, write the person's name and decorate however you wish. (If Mom loves cats, draw a picture of a cat.)

2. On the inside of the place card, write a personal New Year's wish.

ROSH HASHANAH
EVENING

You can make your Rosh Hashanah meal special with opening rituals such as candle lighting, wishes for your children, grape juice or wine, a new fruit, and, of course, round challah dipped in honey.

Visit pjlibrary.org/grow to hear the blessings.

Light the candles and say the blessing.

When saying this Hebrew blessing on Friday night, add the words in parentheses.

LIGHTING THE HOLIDAY CANDLES

Like many Jewish holidays, Rosh Hashanah begins at sundown with lighting candles. As darkness fills the evening sky, glowing candles bring a warm light to the meal inside the house.

בָּרוּךְ אַתָּה יְיָ אֱלֹהֵינוּ מֶלֶךְ הָעוֹלָם אֲשֶׁר קִדְּשָׁנוּ בְּמִצְוֹתָיו וְצִוָּנוּ לְהַדְלִיק נֵר שֶׁל (שַׁבָּת וְשֶׁל) יוֹם טוֹב.

Baruch ata Adonai, Eloheinu melech ha'olam, asher kideshanu bemitzvotav vetzivanu lehadlik ner shel (Shabbat v'shel) yom tov.

Dear God, Creator of our world, thank You for giving us rules that make our lives special and for teaching us to light these holiday candles.

BLESSING THE CHILDREN

The traditional "blessing of the children" is particularly meaningful on Rosh Hashanah, when parents and grandparents can share with their children their hopes and wishes for the new year.

This blessing is 3,000 years old — the oldest Jewish blessing! — and is part of a never-ending chain. Our parents and grandparents (and ancestors before them) blessed us with their actions and qualities, and we carry these blessings forward.

Parents (and grandparents) place their hands on a child's head and say:

יְבָרֶכְךָ יְיָ וְיִשְׁמְרֶךָ.
יָאֵר יְיָ פָּנָיו אֵלֶיךָ וִיחֻנֶּךָּ.
יִשָּׂא יְיָ פָּנָיו אֵלֶיךָ וְיָשֵׂם לְךָ שָׁלוֹם.

Yevarechecha Adonai veyishmerecha.
Ya'er Adonai panav eilecha viyechuneka.
Yisa Adonai panav eilecha veyasem lecha shalom.

May God bless you and keep you safe.
May God's light shine on you and grace your life.
May God turn toward you and give you a world of peace.

Or an alternative version:

Always be safe
Shine light in the world
And feel truly at peace with yourself

Use your PJ Library Never-Ender or visit pjlibrary.org/bless-children.

KIDDUSH

BLESSING OVER WINE OR GRAPE JUICE

בָּרוּךְ אַתָּה יְיָ אֱלֹהֵינוּ מֶלֶךְ הָעוֹלָם בּוֹרֵא פְּרִי הַגָּפֶן.

Baruch ata Adonai, Eloheinu melech ha'olam, borei peri hagafen.

Dear God, Creator of our world, thank You for the delicious fruit that grows on vines.

> The Rosh Hashanah meal begins with a blessing over wine or grape juice with special text focusing on remembrance and history.

בָּרוּךְ אַתָּה יְיָ אֱלֹהֵינוּ מֶלֶךְ הָעוֹלָם אֲשֶׁר בָּחַר בָּנוּ מִכָּל עָם וְרוֹמְמָנוּ מִכָּל לָשׁוֹן וְקִדְּשָׁנוּ בְּמִצְוֹתָיו. וַתִּתֶּן לָנוּ יְיָ אֱלֹהֵינוּ בְּאַהֲבָה אֶת יוֹם (הַשַּׁבָּת הַזֶּה וְאֶת יוֹם) הַזִּכָּרוֹן הַזֶּה יוֹם (זִכְרוֹן) תְּרוּעָה (בְּאַהֲבָה) מִקְרָא קֹדֶשׁ זֵכֶר לִיצִיאַת מִצְרָיִם. כִּי בָנוּ בָחַרְתָּ וְאוֹתָנוּ קִדַּשְׁתָּ מִכָּל הָעַמִּים וּדְבָרְךָ אֱמֶת וְקַיָּם לָעַד. בָּרוּךְ אַתָּה יְיָ מֶלֶךְ עַל כָּל הָאָרֶץ מְקַדֵּשׁ (הַשַּׁבָּת וְ)יִשְׂרָאֵל וְיוֹם הַזִּכָּרוֹן.

Baruch ata Adonai, Eloheinu melech ha'olam, asher bachar banu mikol am, veromemanu mikol lashon, vekideshanu bemitzvotav. Vatiten lanu Adonai Eloheinu b'ahava et yom (haShabbat hazeh v'et yom) haZikaron hazeh, yom (zichron) truah (b'ahava) mikra kodesh, zecher liyetzi'at Mitzrayim. Ki vanu vacharta v'otanu kidashta mikol ha'amim, udevarcha emet vekayam la'ad. Baruch ata Adonai, melech al kol ha'aretz, mekadesh (haShabbat v') Yisra'el veyom haZikaron.

Dear God, Creator of our world, You have given all the people in the world different ways of living and believing. Thank You for giving us the gift of being Jewish and the rules and good deeds that help make us better people. On this day of remembrance — the festival of the shofar's blast — we remember how you took us out of slavery in the land of Egypt. Dear God, thank You for giving us this special day of remembrance to celebrate the New Year.

SHEHECHEYANU

BLESSING FOR REACHING A SPECIAL OCCASION

Jewish tradition offers an important one-line blessing of gratitude: "Thank God we made it to this moment!"

On Rosh Hashanah, it's customary to say this blessing, *Shehecheyanu*, after kiddush, and — as we're welcoming a new year — to accompany it with the eating of a "new fruit," a fruit you haven't eaten in a long time (or maybe have never eaten!).

Say the Shehecheyanu blessing:

בָּרוּךְ אַתָּה יְיָ אֱלֹהֵינוּ מֶלֶךְ הָעוֹלָם
שֶׁהֶחֱיָנוּ וְקִיְּמָנוּ וְהִגִּיעָנוּ לַזְּמַן הַזֶּה.

Baruch ata Adonai, Eloheinu melech ha'olam, shehecheyanu vekiyemanu vehigi'anu lazman hazeh.

Dear God, Creator of our world, thank You for keeping us alive so we can celebrate this important moment.

〉〉 · 〉〉〉 · 〉〉〉 · 〉〉〉 · 〉〉〉 · 〉〉〉 · 〉〉〉 · 〉〉〉 · 〉〉〉 · 〉〉

בָּרוּךְ אַתָּה יְיָ אֱלֹהֵינוּ מֶלֶךְ הָעוֹלָם בּוֹרֵא פְּרִי הָעֵץ.

Baruch ata Adonai, Eloheinu melech ha'olam, borei peri ha'etz.

Dear God, Creator of our world, thank You for fruit that grows on trees.

Pass around the new fruit and say a blessing over fruit (whichever of these two blessings applies).

בָּרוּךְ אַתָּה יְיָ אֱלֹהֵינוּ מֶלֶךְ הָעוֹלָם בּוֹרֵא פְּרִי הָאֲדָמָה.

Baruch ata Adonai, Eloheinu melech ha'olam, borei peri ha'adama.

Dear God, Creator of our world, thank You for fruit that grows in the earth.

NOW TAKE A BITE OF THE NEW FRUIT!

WASHING HANDS & EATING CHALLAH

The round challah of Rosh Hashanah represents many things: wholeness, the round cycle of the year, and a full new year and its blessings. On Shabbat, challah is often dipped in salt. But on Rosh Hashanah, challah is dipped in honey for a sweet new year.

Before eating a meal, it is traditional to wash your hands and say this blessing:

בָּרוּךְ אַתָּה יְיָ אֱלֹהֵינוּ מֶלֶךְ הָעוֹלָם אֲשֶׁר קִדְשָׁנוּ בְּמִצְוֹתָיו וְצִוָּנוּ עַל נְטִילַת יָדָיִם.

Baruch ata Adonai, Eloheinu melech ha'olam, asher kideshanu bemitzvotav vetzivanu al netilat yadayim.

Dear God, Creator of our world, thank You for giving us rules that make our lives special and for teaching us to wash our hands before we eat.

Recite this blessing before you dip the challah in honey and eat it:

בָּרוּךְ אַתָּה יְיָ אֱלֹהֵינוּ מֶלֶךְ הָעוֹלָם הַמּוֹצִיא לֶחֶם מִן הָאָרֶץ.

Baruch ata Adonai, Eloheinu melech ha'olam, hamotzi lechem min ha'aretz.

Dear God, Creator of our world, thank You for bringing bread out of the earth.

SYMBOLIC NEW YEAR FOODS

Welcome to Rosh Hashanah *simanim*
— eating foods with special symbolic value for the new year.
Each of these appetizers is chosen because the food itself (or the
Hebrew name of the food) connects to a wish for the
new year. **Here goes!**

"You're one in a melon!"

"Have a grape New Year!"

APPLES & HONEY — A SWEET NEW YEAR

In ancient Israel, the apple was often eaten as the first dish in
a meal to help spark people's appetite, and honey was a popular
dessert. By dipping an apple in honey, we connect symbols
for the beginning and the end of a meal — symbolizing how one
year is ending and another is beginning.

Take an apple slice, dip it in honey, and say:

יְהִי רָצוֹן מִלְּפָנֶיךָ יְיָ אֱלֹהֵינוּ וֵאלֹהֵי אֲבוֹתֵינוּ
וְאִמּוֹתֵינוּ שֶׁתְּחַדֵּשׁ עָלֵינוּ שָׁנָה טוֹבָה וּמְתוּקָה.

Yehi ratzon milefanecha, Adonai
Eloheinu v'Elohei avoteinu v'imoteinu,
shetechadesh aleinu shanah tovah
u'metukah.

Dear God, renew us for
a good and sweet year.

Now eat a dripping slice of apple!

DATES (Tamar)

HOPING FOR AN END TO HATE

The wordplay here is that the Hebrew word **tam** means "end." The wish for the new year is that hatred in our world will end. Say the blessing, then eat a date.

יְהִי רָצוֹן מִלְּפָנֶיךָ יְיָ אֱלֹהֵינוּ וֵאלֹהֵי אֲבוֹתֵינוּ וְאִמּוֹתֵינוּ שֶׁיִּתַּמּוּ אוֹיְבֵינוּ וְשׂוֹנְאֵינוּ וְכָל מְבַקְשֵׁי רָעָתֵנוּ.

Yehi ratzon milefanecha, Adonai Eloheinu v'Elohei avoteinu v'imoteinu, sheyi**tam**u oyveinu veson'einu vechol mevakshei ra'ateinu.

Dear God, in this new year, please end all hatred.

CARROT (Gezer)

WISHING FOR A GOOD JUDGMENT

The pun here is that **gezer** also means a firm decision or judgment. The wish is that we will be judged favorably in this High Holiday season. Say the blessing, then crunch some carrots (or eat them quietly if they're cooked).

יְהִי רָצוֹן מִלְּפָנֶיךָ יְיָ אֱלֹהֵינוּ וֵאלֹהֵי אֲבוֹתֵינוּ וְאִמּוֹתֵינוּ שֶׁתִּגְזוֹר עָלֵינוּ גְּזֵרוֹת טוֹבוֹת.

Yehi ratzon milefanecha, Adonai Eloheinu v'Elohei avoteinu v'imoteinu, shetigzor aleinu **gezer**ot tovot.

Dear God, in this new year, please give us a good judgment.

POMEGRANATE (Rimon)

FILLING UP WITH GOOD DEEDS

The hundreds of seeds inside a pomegranate represent the many good deeds — *mitzvot* — we can do to make the world better. Say the blessing, then eat some seeds. (Watch out for stains …)

יְהִי רָצוֹן מִלְּפָנֶיךָ יְיָ אֱלֹהֵינוּ וֵאלֹהֵי אֲבוֹתֵינוּ וְאִמוֹתֵינוּ שֶׁנִּהְיֶה מְלֵאִים מִצְווֹת כְּרִמּוֹן.

Yehi ratzon milefanecha, Adonai Eloheinu v'Elohei avoteinu v'imoteinu, shenih'yeh melei'im mitzvot ke**rimon**.

Dear God, in this new year, may our good deeds be as many as the seeds of a pomegranate.

✀ ✀ ✀ ✀ ✀ ✀ ✀ ✀ ✀

Your family may prefer to use a suggestion of a fish head (fish-shaped crackers or a gummy fish) or a different kind of "head" entirely — a head of lettuce, cabbage, broccoli, cauliflower, or an artichoke.

✀ ✀ ✀

"HEAD OF THE YEAR"

Finally, we hope that on Rosh Hashanah ("head of the year") we will hold our heads up high and be leaders for others. Traditionally, this blessing was said with a fish head (!), but it can be said instead with another symbolic "head."

יְהִי רָצוֹן מִלְּפָנֶיךָ יְיָ אֱלֹהֵינוּ וֵאלֹהֵי אֲבוֹתֵינוּ וְאִמוֹתֵינוּ שֶׁנִּהְיֶה לְרֹאשׁ וְלֹא לְזָנָב.

Yehi ratzon milefanecha, Adonai Eloheinu v'Elohei avoteinu v'imoteinu, shenih'yeh le**rosh** velo lezanav.

Dear God, in this new year, may we be like the head and not the tail.

If your family is inspired by the Jewish tradition of *simanim* (symbols) to create your own food symbolism, go for it! Think what foods could represent values you want to highlight in the new year. (If you're brave, create some English-language puns to go along with them.)

And now, enjoy your holiday meal.

ROSH HASHANAH DAY

WHAT'S ALL THE PRAYING ABOUT?

UNPACKING 5 HIGH HOLIDAY PRAYERS

Jewish prayers are hundreds and even thousands of years old — chanted poems, usually addressed to God, that can inspire us to feel things and wish for things that are deep and important.

But for many people, praying isn't so simple. Who are we talking to, and is anybody listening? Why so many words and so much Hebrew?

The key is to approach prayer with an open heart and mind. On Rosh Hashanah and Yom Kippur, prayers can act as special "messengers" that carry ideas both into our hearts and out to the universe. Prayers can help us think about how we want to improve ourselves and our world.

The Hebrew word for "pray" is LEHITPALEL, which means "to judge ourselves." On the High Holidays that is exactly what we do when we pray.

FAMILY-FRIENDLY PRAYERS

The prayers on the following pages are shortened and translated to be family friendly. You can read the prayers out loud and discuss them as a family.

Hear them sung at pjlibrary.org/grow.

And remember, you can always follow an ancient Jewish tradition: Find your own words to express your hopes and feelings.

TALKING WITH YOUR KIDS ABOUT GOD

 BY RABBI AVI KILLIP

PERSONAL STORY

My littlest brother is the youngest of four. (We are each one year apart.) Once, when he was very little and was asked about the ages in our family, he reported, "Hana is 5, Avi is 4, Aaron is 3, I am 2, and God is 1." He had absorbed the teaching from our nightly bedtime *Shema*, which said "...the Lord our God, the Lord is One." So my brother understood God as part of our family — as his 1-year-old younger sibling.

Even if we don't say a prayer every night or even talk about it at all, our children develop an understanding of God at a very young age. Without our ever raising the subject, they learn — from Jewish rituals and songs and from general society. And, profoundly, many children feel spirituality through their own experiences of the world, developing their own personal connections to the divine.

Teaching our children about God can feel scary and even impossible. How can we teach our children something we ourselves don't understand? Maybe most importantly: How can we stay open to the idea that our children's experiences of God and spirituality might be different from ours?

I may feel no relationship with God and find myself parenting a deeply spiritual child.

There is no need to be intimidated by this. You don't have to have a robust spiritual life in order to cultivate and nourish one in your child.

So, instead of asking how we can talk <u>to</u> our kids about God, let's instead ask how we can encourage their curiosity and listen to their questions with open hearts.

If you do have your own connection, your own spiritual journey, you can invite your children in by modeling. Let your children watch you pray, whether that prayer is a traditional Hebrew one or a few lines spoken from your heart before bed, while lighting candles on Shabbat, or in a particularly difficult moment.

Whether you are standing at a waterfall, gazing up at the stars, or holding your newborn nephew, when you feel something is holy or sacred, invite your children into those moments by telling them what you feel.

And when you have questions and doubts about God, you can share them too — invite your children into the questions.

You will have many chances to talk with your children about God, so there's no pressure to get it all right or have all the answers. The questions they ask will evolve over time.

As parents, we sometimes find ourselves in these deep conversations at the most unexpected moments, whenever our child's mind or heart generates questions — while brushing teeth, maybe in the grocery store. There is no wrong place or time to engage.

But if you are looking for a way in, grab a PJ Library book off your shelf. Read together and start a conversation

PROMPTS FOR KIDS AND PARENTS

One thing I have always wondered about God is ...

Have you ever witnessed something miraculous or truly amazing? Share the story of how you felt.

What would you say if you knew God was listening?

See where the conversation takes you. Remember, you can always answer a child's question with a question of your own.

"WE ARE ALL CHILDREN"

DURING ROSH HASHANAH, the "birthday of the world," we pause to admire how beautiful, big, and mysterious our world is. We also recognize the many things we cannot control that can make us feel small and powerless.

In that spirit, a special prayer — *Avinu Malkeinu* (ah-VEE-noo mahl-KAY-noo) — speaks to God in the voice of a child asking a parent for help. (Sometimes even grown-ups feel a bit like children.) People of all ages stand together and ask to be loved, forgiven for their mistakes, protected from danger, and inspired to do better.

A short version of this prayer was first spoken nearly 2,000 years ago by Rabbi Akiva in Jerusalem. Over the centuries, it was further developed by Jews in Iraq, France, Poland, Syria, and beyond.

FAMILY REFLECTION

WHAT WISH WOULD YOU LIKE TO ADD TO AVINU MALKEINU?

AVINU MALKEINU — OUR PARENT, OUR SUPPORT

Avinu Malkeinu, hear our voice — *sh'ma koleinu*

Avinu Malkeinu, we have made mistakes — *hatanu lefanecha*

Avinu Malkeinu, forgive us and our family — *hamol aleinu ve'al olaleinu vetapeinu*

Avinu Malkeinu, let the new year be a good year — *hadesh aleinu shanah tovah*

Avinu Malkeinu, make an end to disease, violence, and hunger — *kalei dever veherev vera'av mei'aleinu*

Avinu Malkeinu, send healing to all sick people — *shlach refua shleima leholei amecha*

Avinu Malkeinu, put an end to unfairness — *kalei kol tzar umastin mei'aleinu*

Avinu Malkeinu, give strength to the Jewish people — *hareim keren Yisrael amecha*

Avinu Malkeinu, write us for a blessing in the Book of Life — *kotveinu besefer hayim tovim*

Avinu Malkeinu, help us all grow into our best selves — *hatzmach lanu yeshua bekarov*

Avinu Malkeinu, please answer us, though we may not deserve it, and treat us generously and kindly and help us to improve — *Haneinu va'aneinu ki ein banu ma'asim. Asei imanu tzedakah vachesed vehoshi'einu.*

This next prayer — *Ki Anu Amecha* (kee AH-nu ah-MEH-cha) — is recited on Yom Kippur and uses different images to describe the relationship between humans and the divine, including the image of children reaching out to a parent.

KI ANU AMECHA — BECAUSE WE ARE YOUR PEOPLE

Ki anu amecha ve'ata Eloheinu —
Because we are your people, and you are our God

Anu vanecha ve'ata avinu —
We are your children, and you are our parent

Anu karmecha ve'ata notreinu —
We are your crops, and you are our farmer

Anu tzonecha ve'ata ro'einu —
We are your flock, and you are our shepherd

Anu k'shei oref ve'ata erech apayim —
We are stubborn, while you are patient

Anu fe'ulatecha ve'ata yotzreinu —
We are a piece of artwork, and you are the artist

"WE TAKE RESPONSIBILITY"

During the High Holidays, we talk openly about the things we have done in the past year and how to improve our actions in the future. A prayer called *Ashamnu* (ah-SHAHM-noo) gives a long list of mistakes we have made. It is recited in a group out loud because everyone makes mistakes.

In the synagogue on Yom Kippur, the whole community says the prayer together, and at home the whole family can say it together. While speaking each line of the prayer, it is a tradition to tap your fist over your heart, as if to say, "Open up, heart, so in the new year we can be more kind and loving."

ASHAMNU — WE TAKE RESPONSIBILITY

We take responsibility (*ashamnu*) for times when …

We hid things from others — *bagadnu*

We took something that wasn't ours — *gazalnu*

We said something bad about others — *dibarnu dofi*

We got someone else into trouble — *hirshanu*

We told a lie — *tafalnu shaker*

We made fun of someone — *latznu*

We disobeyed our parents — *maradnu*

We were not always kind to our friends — *tzararnu*

We refused to admit that we were wrong — *kishinu oref*

We hit or hurt someone — *rashanu*

We did something we knew we shouldn't — *shihatnu*

We weren't thinking and just messed up — *ta'inu*

As we start a new year, forgive us for our mistakes and give us a chance to be better.

Slach lanu. Mechal lanu. Kaper lanu. Clean our slate, wipe away the bad, help us learn and grow.

FAMILY REFLECTION

WHICH MISTAKES FROM THE LIST DO WE WANT TO WORK ON MOST THIS YEAR?

DON'T FORGET According to Jewish tradition, it's fine to ask God for forgiveness, but that doesn't help fix mistakes you've made with another person. For that, you need to talk directly to that person and work things out.

A POSITIVE ASHAMNU

As we take responsibility for mistakes we have made, we can also celebrate the positive things we do. In recent years, people have begun to recite a version of *Ashamnu* that helps us remember all the healthy behavior we want to continue in the new year.

Ahavnu — We loved

Beirachnu — We blessed

Gadalnu — We grew

Diminu yofi — We made beautiful things

Hitakashnu — We pushed on

Vitarnu — We compromised

Zar'anu — We planted

Hipasnu — We explored

Tiharnu sheker — We told the truth

Yatzarnu — We created

Ka'avnu — We felt others' pain

Lamadnu — We learned

Mahalnu – We gave someone a break

Nisinu — We kept trying

Salachnu — We forgave

Azarnu — We helped out

Pirganu — We showed appreciation

Tzahaknu — We laughed

Kibalnu — We accepted

Radafnu tzedek — We demanded fairness

Samachnu — We felt joy

Taramnu — We contributed

Tamachnu — We supported

Tikanu — We fixed

FAMILY REFLECTION

WHAT WOULD YOU ADD TO THIS LIST?

"WE TUNE INTO THE POWER OF THIS DAY"

The prayer below — *Unetaneh Tokef* (oo-neh-TAH-neh TOE-kef) — is one of the most famous prayers of Rosh Hashanah and Yom Kippur. It describes a scene where God is looking at each human being during the High Holidays, and considering what they did in the past year and what will happen to them in the new year.

What will be decided? We cannot know. Each year shows how uncertain the future is for all human beings. When this prayer imagines a judge in a divine courtroom, it inspires us to do our own self-reflection. The shofar calls on us to tune into the moment and ask: What have we done — and what will we do?

The original source of the prayer is unclear, but it was likely written in Israel more than 1,400 years ago. More recently, it served as the inspiration for Leonard Cohen's well-known song "Who by Fire."

UNETANEH TOKEF
WE TUNE INTO THE POWER OF THIS DAY

We tune into the sacred power of this day, a day that is both amazing and a little scary. The shofar makes a blast, and we hear a small, still voice. The angels are saying, "This is the day of taking stock, when The Holy One looks into the soul of every person."

On Rosh Hashanah the judgment is written down, and on the fast of Yom Kippur it is sealed:

Who will live and who will die

Who will live a long life and who will not

Who will be calm and who will be restless

Who will have plenty and who will be in need

Who will reach their goals and who will fall short

By tuning into the sacred power of this day, opening our hearts, and working for a better world, we hope to be judged with kindness.

FAMILY REFLECTION

HOW DO YOU TUNE INTO THE POWER OF THE HIGH HOLIDAYS?

HOW ARE YOU THINKING ABOUT THE YEAR THAT JUST FINISHED AND THE YEAR AHEAD?

"WE ARE CALLED TO PRAISE"

Composed in Babylonia about 1,800 years ago, the prayer *Aleinu* (ah-LAY-noo) is said every day of the year. But on the High Holidays, we do something special when reciting it. While saying a few special words, we bend our knees to the ground and stretch our upper body forward so our forehead touches the floor.

When we go into this stretched-out pose, we are putting our whole bodies into our hope for a good new year. We are giving everything we have. We are showing that we are but one small part of a huge and interconnected world.

Bending our knees and our backs is also a reminder that we need to be flexible. If we are too stiff and stubborn, we can never improve ourselves and change as the world around us changes. Indeed, Aleinu is a Jewish prayer for a changing world — that one day, fear and hatred will completely disappear.

As you prepare to say the prayer as a family, find a place where each person can stretch out during the middle of the prayer.

FAMILY REFLECTION

HOW DO YOU WANT TO STRETCH YOURSELF IN THE NEW YEAR?

ALEINU — WE ARE CALLED TO PRAISE

With our unique story and special values
we are called as the Jewish people
to praise the Creator of all things.

Bend down to the ground and stretch your body forward.

So we bend our knees, bow down to the ground,
and say out loud how grateful we are.
Stand back up.

And we hope, Source of Unity, that you will
help us fix the world
and make it whole.

TASHLICH

CASTING AWAY OUR MISTAKES

We can apologize for times when we did not act nicely. But we cannot make those times disappear. They happened. We take responsibility for them and then move forward.

Rosh Hashanah has a special cleansing ceremony called *tashlich*, which means to "cast" or "throw away." It is a chance to symbolically get rid of our bad actions.

For tashlich, typically practiced on Rosh Hashanah afternoon, people gather by a flowing body of water — a pond, river, ocean, well, or backyard fish pond. (If no flowing water is accessible, a bucket of water will do.) We throw breadcrumbs into the water. The pieces of bread represent bad actions from last year that we want to leave behind. The water represents the life flow inside all living things, the source of cleansing.

HAVE YOU TRIED THIS?

BRING SOME OLD PIECES OF BREAD TO A BODY OF WATER.

Take turns throwing crumbs into the water.

If you like, read this passage from the Bible, traditionally said at tashlich:

God does not stay angry forever, for God prefers love and kindness.

God, return to us, forgive us, and cover over our bad actions from the past. Cast into the depths of the sea all of our bad actions. (Prophet Micah 7:18-19)

If it feels right, use tashlich as an occasion to talk about your mistakes (the ones you were thinking about as you threw your crumbs) and ways to grow and improve.

A TWIST ON TASHLICH

Bread isn't healthy for all animals, and some communities discourage throwing food into rivers and streams. While bread is customary, there are other ways to cast your mistakes away. Try these twists on tradition:

SMALL PEBBLES
The trick with stones is to toss them gently, making sure no one is in the stone's path.

 **BITS OF LEAVES**
or flower petals, pine needles, or something else that already exists in your ecosystem.

No matter what you decide to toss, remember that tashlich — in the words of PJ Library author April Halprin Wayland — is like "cleaning your heart's closet." Think about things you regret having said or done, then let them go.

WASHING AWAY & LETTING GO

In the spirit of tashlich, here are additional activities to do during this season to help us "wash away" our mistakes and "let go" of bad actions.

HANDS ON!

MAKE A "LETTING GO" COLLAGE

Here's an idea: Turn your mistakes into art!

SUPPLIES

PEN OR MARKER

COLORFUL/PATTERNED PAPER

SCISSORS

GLUE

LARGE PIECE OF POSTER BOARD

Anytime you need to say sorry to someone for something you've done wrong, do your best to make it right. Then write or draw a picture of it on a small piece of colorful paper (for example, "I didn't share my toy with my sister"). Cut the paper into small pieces so that you can't read the words anymore. Glue these pieces onto the poster board in any design you like. Continue to add different colored paper each time, letting go of your mistakes as you create something new and beautiful.

HANDS ON!

"WASH" MISTAKES AWAY

On Rosh Hashanah we begin to think about mistakes we've made in the past year. Here's a craft that lets you "wash away" those mistakes!

SUPPLIES

WASHABLE MARKERS

EXTRA-LARGE COFFEE FILTERS

Use the washable markers to draw pictures on the coffee filters of things that you are sorry for and don't want to repeat in the new year. As you draw, reflect on these mistakes and resolve to do better. Take the filters to the sink or bathtub, place them in water, and watch the mistakes wash away.

YOU CAN ALSO TRY THESE VARIATIONS:

Use bath crayons to write or draw things in the bathtub that you're sorry about and then wash them away.

Use sidewalk chalk to make a short list of things you're sorry about. Then use water to "erase" the words and sentences in the list.

THE TEN DAYS OF RETURNING

THE NEW YEAR HAS BEGUN

The ten days beginning with Rosh Hashanah and ending with Yom Kippur are called the Ten Days of **Teshuvah** (Ten Days of Returning) — turning away from our mistakes and returning to the "best self" we can be.

We have a special opportunity to focus on our relationships, to say we're sorry for things we've done wrong, and to discuss how to make our connections to family, friends, and community stronger.

Many Jewish thinkers have asked how we know when we're really sorry and that we've really changed. The answer is simple. When you're in the same situation again — a situation in which you previously made a bad choice or behaved poorly — this time you get it right. <u>That's</u> teshuvah.

Of course, no one turns completely around in ten days. The Ten Days of Returning are meant to jump-start a process that continues year-round. It's a chance to make a good beginning. You can have honest conversations. You can apologize and offer forgiveness. You can take important first steps — helping at home, not losing your cool, communicating with friends and family, giving *tzedakah* (charitable donations).

Here are conversation starters to help you on your way.

At the back of the guide you'll find these questions in a **worksheet format** to tear out for one-time use or photocopy each year.

Use the questions on the following pages to guide you.

Turn to the back
of the book to fill out your
own answers or download
more copies online at
pjlibrary.org/grow.

FAMILY CONVERSATIONS

The Ten Days (including Rosh Hashanah and Yom Kippur)
are a good time for having thoughtful one-on-one
conversations or a sit-down talk as a whole family.
You can use these prompts to guide you.

Think about
your actions.

1. MAKING MYSELF (EVEN) BETTER

What things have I done this past year that I'm proud of?

What can I do this new year that I'll be proud of?

How can I get started?

Have a one-on-one
conversation with a
family member or
friend.

2. MAKING FAMILY AND FRIENDSHIPS STRONGER

What are some kind things we've done for each other this past year?

How have we disrespected or hurt each other this past
year? Now is the time to apologize for those acts and
to offer each other forgiveness.

What's the best way to keep these things from
happening again?

3. FAMILY GOALS

When do we feel most connected as a family? When is it harder to get along?

How can we support each other better?

What are some ideas for making family time more special in the new year?

Sit as a family to discuss your goals for the new year and ways to grow even kinder to each other.

As a family, discuss ways to reach out to others in your neighborhood, your community, and the world.

4. FIXING THE WORLD (tikkun olam in Hebrew)

Do we have a neighbor who lives alone or friends who are going through a difficult time? What can we do to help them?

Are there people in our community who need food, clothes, or shelter? Are there people who aren't treated fairly? What are some ways we can support them?

What are our tikkun olam goals (helping animals, helping the environment, visiting the elderly, etc.) and what project ideas can we think up?

If your family has a tzedakah box for collecting money for charitable donations, this is a good time of year to talk about where to give the money when the box gets full.

YOM KIPPUR

The Ten Days of Returning end with *Yom Kippur* (YOHM kee-POOR), an entire day set aside for thinking about our actions of the past year and how to improve in the new year.

Yom Kippur is a community experience. Millions of Jewish people are spending the day doing the same thing. The prayers for Yom Kippur talk about mistakes <u>we</u> have made, because on this day everyone stands together, even when apart. All of us, young and old, make mistakes, and we all deserve a second chance.

So while Yom Kippur can be challenging, we end the day feeling happy and relieved, knowing we're making a fresh start in a new year with a chance to be an even better person.

This is a perfect day for asking: What is my best self? How can I keep growing toward that?

WHAT'S IN THE PICTURE?

A DIFFERENT DAY

Take a few minutes to look at this Yom Kippur scene. Turn the page for explanations.

WHAT'S IN THE PICTURE?

EMPTY PLATE.
Many grown-ups and older children don't eat or drink on Yom Kippur. That's called fasting, and the full fast is from sundown (beginning of Yom Kippur) to nightfall the next day (end of Yom Kippur) — 25 hours! Some people find they enter a different zone when they fast, where they can think more deeply about their life and actions. Kids don't usually fast, but you can choose other ways to make the day feel different.

STAYING FOCUSED.
Yom Kippur is a time for mindfulness, for reflection on our lives and deeds. Where is a special place outside or in your home where you can focus best? What can you do to create a calm mood for thinking and sharing?

WHITE CLOTHES.
On Yom Kippur some people wear white shirts or dresses. It's a symbol of making a fresh start. What special clothes will you wear on Yom Kippur?

Have an easy fast!

YOM KIPPUR GREETING.
When we see people on Yom Kippur, we can say "*Tzom kal*" (tzohm kahl), which means, "I hope your fast isn't too hard!" We can also say "*G'mar hatimah tovah*" (ge-MAHR hah-tee-MAH toe-VAH), which means, "I hope a good judgment is sealed for you in the Book of Life." When Yom Kippur is over, we simply say "*Shanah tovah*" — "Have a good year!"

TZEDAKAH BOX.
On this day we think about people who go hungry <u>every day</u>, not just on Yom Kippur. In the days before Yom Kippur, we can help others by collecting coins in a tzedakah box. What can your coins be used for?

FINAL PREPARATION

Tips before beginning Yom Kippur

TAKE A SHOWER. It's traditional not to shower on Yom Kippur, so some people shower right before the fast begins. On a day when we're thinking about cleaning ourselves on the <u>inside</u>, it's nice to start clean on the outside.

EAT A GOOD MEAL TOGETHER. The meal eaten before the Yom Kippur fast is a festive "separation" meal, and it's traditional to eat challah dipped in honey, just like on Rosh Hashanah. Even if you're not fasting, take time at this meal to appreciate how important food is.

PLAN AHEAD. Kids aren't expected to fast, but you might want to choose something you'll do differently on Yom Kippur.

Some ideas for things not to do: Don't do household chores. (That's easy.) Don't eat dessert. (That's harder.)

Some ideas for things <u>to do</u>: Read a book. Take a walk outside — in nature, if possible. Talk about ways you can change in the new year. Pray or meditate — whatever that means for you. Play quietly. Do some of the suggested activities on the following pages, either as preparation for Yom Kippur or on Yom Kippur itself, depending on your family's practice.

YOM KIPPUR

EVENING

KOL NIDREI
HOW WE OPEN YOM KIPPUR

When families go to synagogue on the evening of Yom Kippur, everyone begins by standing.

We open the ark and take out the Torah scrolls. We sing a powerful melody called *Kol Nidrei* (All Our Vows) and ask to be forgiven for mistakes we've made in the past year. We sing *Avinu Malkeinu* — also sung on Rosh Hashanah — and call out for healing (*refuah*), fairness (*tzedakah*), and compassion (*chesed*).

At home, your family may want to enter the spirit of Yom Kippur with music or prayers, with stories or quiet conversation. You can pick a PJ Library or PJ Our Way book you like. (Can you find one in which a character has the courage to change?) You can read selected prayers together (pages 24–31 in this guide) and hear songs and prayers at **pjlibrary.org/grow**. If your family hasn't found time for Family Conversations (pages 77–80 in this guide), now is a great time to sit and talk.

YOM KIPPUR DAY

COVERING OVER & PLANTING NEW

Kippur comes from a Hebrew root meaning "covering over." So Yom Kippur is the "day of covering over." We can picture in our minds covering our bad actions from the previous year and planting seeds in the soil for the new year. But how do we "cover over" bad habits and make better ones?

We can start by looking more closely at some of the habits we want to change. Here are a few simple activities that can help.

Do you ever get frustrated and lose your temper? Try the activity on the right.

HANDS ON!

CREATE A WHEEL OF CHOICES

Conflicts arise in all relationships, and feeling angry is natural. Some reactions are more helpful than others. Practice dealing with these feelings by creating a Wheel of Choices.

SUPPLIES

LARGE PIECE OF PAPER OR POSTER BOARD

MARKERS OR CRAYONS

On the paper or poster board, draw a big circle and divide it into wedges, like a pie (make sure the pieces are large enough to write and draw on).

Think of different things you can do when you're angry to help you calm down and make good choices. Options might include dancing it out, taking deep breaths, counting down slowly from 10, running to your favorite quiet place in your house or yard, calling a friend — whatever works for you.

Write each of your actions on a piece of the wheel and draw a picture to go along with it. Consult the wheel for help the next time you feel angry!

Have you ever thought of a different way you could have acted — a "different ending" you could have chosen to a situation? Try the activities below!

Do you ever have trouble expressing your feelings?

HANDS ON!

WRITE THE NEXT PAGE

On a few pieces of paper, write about and draw a situation in which you made a mistake and hurt someone's feelings. What did you do? How did you make the person feel? Take one or two sheets of paper and write a new ending to this story. What could you have done differently? Or what can you do to make things better?

HANDS ON!

ROLE PLAY WITH STUFFIES

Children can learn about compassion and empathy by acting out scenarios with toys and stuffed animals.

Gather stuffed animals and introduce your child to them one by one. Explain what problem each critter has; perhaps Elephant is hungry or Penguin has a hurt wing. Allow your child to create solutions to solve the toys' problems. Make sure each stuffie remembers to say "thank you!"

THE STORY OF JONAH

It's traditional on Yom Kippur afternoon to read the biblical story of Jonah. Here is a modern retelling.

What do we have in common with Jonah? When Jonah doesn't want to do something, he feels like running away!

One day God says to Jonah that people in a far-off city are treating each other badly. Jonah should stop what he's doing, go there, and tell the people to change their behavior.

Jonah says to himself, "No thank you. I'm not getting involved." He boards a boat sailing in the opposite direction.

Unfortunately for Jonah, God makes the sea stormy. The sailors realize that Jonah has angered God by running away. When they ask Jonah how to make the seas calm again, Jonah insists that they throw him overboard.

Before Jonah has a chance to swim, a giant whale comes along and swallows him. From inside the whale's belly, Jonah prays to God. When the whale spits Jonah out onto land, Jonah knows that he must do what God told him to do in the first place.

Jonah travels to this far-off city and speaks out. He tells the residents that they must treat each other kindly. They take Jonah's message to heart and begin to change, and God forgives them.

Jonah says to God: "Really? You forgive them, just like that?"

The answer is yes. Everyone has the power to forgive. Everyone can show compassion and kindness to others.

FAMILY REFLECTION

WHEN HAVE YOU RUN AWAY FROM RESPONSIBILITY?

WHEN HAVE YOU CALLED SOMEONE OUT FOR ACTING BADLY?

WHEN HAVE YOU FORGIVEN SOMEONE?

GOALS & CHALLENGES FOR THE NEW YEAR

Yom Kippur has a unique rhythm all its own. When we begin Yom Kippur, our focus is on different ways we've messed up in the past year. As the day goes on, the focus shifts, and we imagine ourselves growing into better people. We imagine the world as a better place, with each of us playing an important role.

Here are some activities that challenge us to be our best selves — to be kind to our family, to encourage others and ourselves, and to set goals for the new year.

HANDS ON!

MAKE YOUR OWN STICKY-NOTE WALL

No one likes chores, but everyone likes gift certificates. So create a sticky-note wall for your family, and help each other out with sticky-note "gift certificates."

SUPPLIES

STICKY NOTES

PEN

Here's how it works. When someone in your family does something nice for you, pay it forward. Have everyone write small chores ("take out garbage" or "feed dog") on sticky notes and place them on the fridge. The next time someone can lend a hand to help out, they can choose a sticky note, and the job will get done — with a smile!

HANDS ON!

CREATE A KINDNESS WHEEL

Yom Kippur is a great time to think about ways to show kindness to the people we care about. Here's a craft to help encourage the process.

SUPPLIES

MARKER OR CRAYON

PAPER PLATE

SCISSORS

PIECE OF THIN CARDBOARD

BRASS PAPER FASTENER

Using the marker or crayon, divide the back of the paper plate into pie-shaped wedges. Write one person's name inside each wedge. Cut an arrow shape out of the thin cardboard and use the brass fastener to attach it to the center of the plate. Spin the arrow, see whose name it lands on, and then decide on an act of kindness to do for that person. Repeat often.

MAKE ENCOURAGEMENT STONES

Everyone can shine in the new year — with a little encouragement. Show family and friends that you're supporting them, and maybe offer yourself some encouragement too. Here's how.

SUPPLIES

NEWSPAPER

NONTOXIC ACRYLIC PAINT

PAINTBRUSHES

STONES (LARGE, FLAT SURFACES ARE IDEAL)

OIL-BASED PAINT PEN (OPTIONAL BUT HELPFUL)

Spread newspaper over your painting surface, then paint the stones however you like. Once dry, use a fine-tipped paintbrush or paint pen to write encouraging messages like "Keep it up!" or "You can do it!" Then give the stones to friends and family who could use an encouraging word.

MAKE A VISION BOARD

Jonah finds himself inside the belly of a whale because he is running away from challenges. A vision board can help you visualize the challenges you face and set goals to deal with them head on. What better time to do that than the start of the Jewish New Year?

SUPPLIES

POSTER BOARD

OLD MAGAZINES

SCISSORS

GLUE

Start with a large piece of poster board (optional: cut it into the shape of a whale!). As you flip through the magazines, cut out images of things that relate to your own personal goals and challenges. Glue the images onto the poster board.

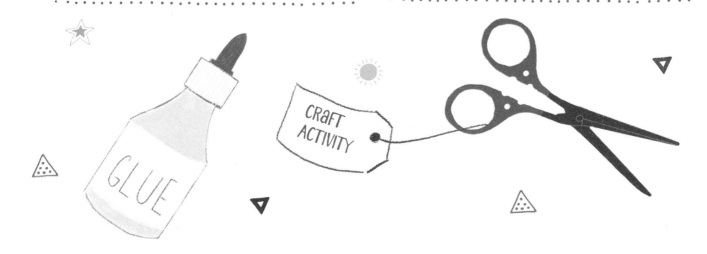

CRAFT ACTIVITY

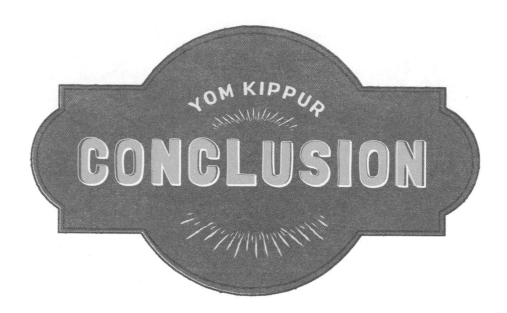

CLOSING THE GATE & ENDING THE FAST

Yom Kippur ends at nightfall, when three stars appear in the sky. Go outside together as a family, and see who finds three stars first.

When we're at synagogue and the end of Yom Kippur approaches, there's a lot of action. The ark is opened up, and sometimes people are invited to go right up to the ark and say their own private prayer (kids too!). It's like our last chance to say what's in our hearts before the gates of heaven, which are open wide for Yom Kippur, close up at the end of the day.

Finally, we hear the loud blast of the shofar piercing the air, signaling the end of the holiday and the fast.

SOUND THE SHOFAR

If you have a shofar at home (or have made your own), you can blow it for yourself to mark the end of Yom Kippur:

Tekiah Gedolah — blow the shofar and hold it as long as you can.

Blow along with Jewish people all over the world. Make it long and loud! Blow for a sweet new year, full of love and good deeds, justice and happiness for everyone.

A BITE OF FOOD

And then, for anyone who has been fasting (and even if you're not), a bite of food — a first little nosh. How good does that taste?

Now that Yom Kippur has ended, you can have a festive meal as a family — a break-the-fast meal that traditionally resembles breakfast! Many people have lighter foods, like bagels, cream cheese, and fruit, so it's not too much of a shock to their stomachs after a day of fasting (But of course, a little ice cream never hurts.) Talk as a family about how it feels to start the year with a clean slate.

SUKKOT

Five days after Yom Kippur, the moon grows full. It lights up a special celebration called **Sukkot** (soo-COAT), a harvest festival that lasts for an entire week. Sukkot is known as "the time of our joy." On Sukkot we celebrate completing the hard work of *teshuvah* (turning ourselves around). Now we can relax and embrace life's simple joys.

Sukkot literally means "small huts." For the week of Sukkot, it is a tradition to build a **sukkah** (hut) outdoors to relive experiences from the Jewish past. These include the desert encampments of the Israelites fleeing slavery in Egypt, the field tents used by farmers in ancient Israel during the fall harvest, and the tents of pilgrims visiting the Holy Temple in Jerusalem.

For seven days, the sukkah becomes our temporary home for eating, relaxing, and even sleeping. We hang fruits and vegetables in the sukkah and are grateful for the plenty in our lives. We gaze at the stars and think about our connection with our beautiful world. Sitting outside of our home (and all the stuff it holds) helps us focus on the blessing of being together with family, friends, and community.

**In this new year, what will give you joy?
What are you thankful for?**

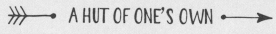

A HUT OF ONE'S OWN

Take a few minutes to look at this Sukkot scene. What special things do you notice? Turn the page for explanations.

WHAT'S IN THE PICTURE?

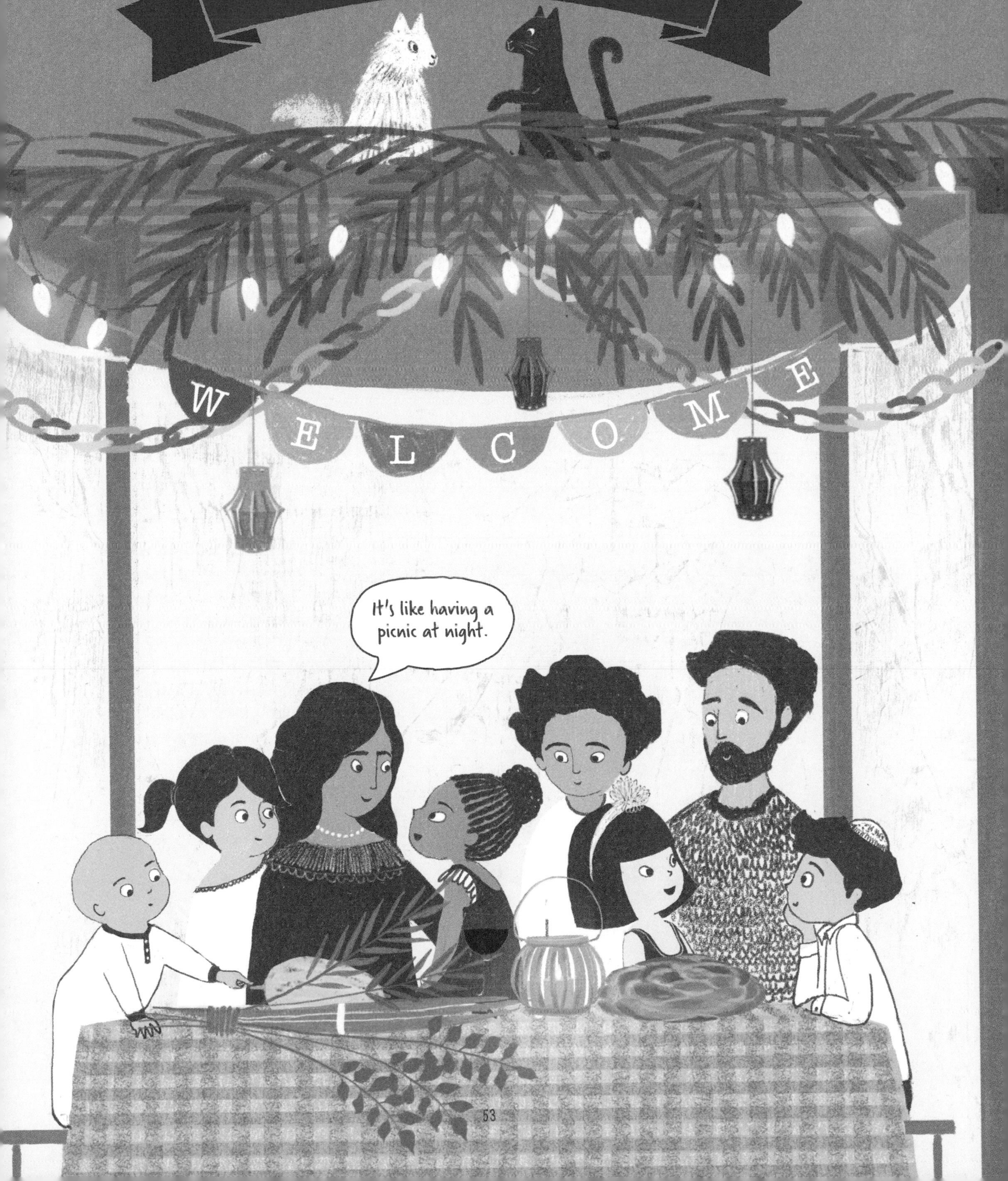

WHAT'S IN THE PICTURE?

TIME TO DECORATE
One of the best parts of preparing a sukkah is decorating it. Popular decorations include fruits and gourds hanging on string, colorful paper chains, homemade pictures, lanterns and other lights, and seasonal foliage and flowers.

GET IN THE FRAME
The sukkah hut is built outdoors with a rectangular frame of wood or metal and walls of fabric or wood. It has an opening on at least one side. Putting up a sukkah can be as fun as eating in one. To learn where to buy a sukkah kit or make your own family sukkah, visit **pjlibrary.org/sukkot**. (If you can't build a sukkah outdoors, see the next page for an indoor version.)

STARRY, STARRY NIGHT
The roof of a sukkah consists of natural materials: tree branches, bamboo poles, corn stalks, or plants grown from the ground. This covering — called *s'chach* in Hebrew — should provide shade from the sun yet still allow you to see the stars at night.

IF LIFE GIVES YOU AN ETROG ...
A unique sukkot ritual is shaking a *lulav* (loo-LAHV) — a combination of a palm branch and willow and myrtle boughs — alongside a lemonlike citron called an *etrog* (eh-TROGUE). Waving around this unusual plant-and-fruit combination is an ancient tradition with special meaning. See page 58 to learn more.

WELCOME

YOU'RE WELCOME!
Inviting guests to join a meal inside the sukkah is a special part of the holiday. In addition to setting out extra chairs for visitors, you may want to design a homemade welcome sign to greet guests.

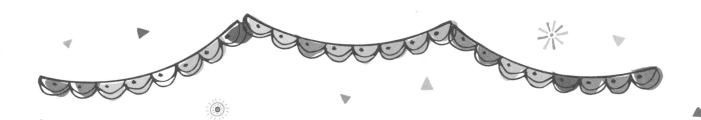

MAKE A MINI PLAY SUKKAH

Kids can enjoy celebrating Sukkot with their own minisukkah.

SUPPLIES

CARDBOARD BOX

SCISSORS

SMALL LEAFY BRANCHES

CRAFT SUPPLIES (MARKERS, PAINT, OR STICKERS)

Cut the flaps off one side of your cardboard box. Turn the box on its side so the open side faces you, then cut off the top panel. Lay small branches across the top opening to create a roof of s'chach. Decorate the sukkah with craft supplies. Now invite friends! A minisukkah can accommodate stuffed animal guests, and a larger one is the perfect place to hang out with the human kind. Enjoy being together!

MAKE A SUKKAH-FORT

A sukkah-fort is the perfect place to practice Sukkot hospitality.

SUPPLIES

CHAIRS

COUCH CUSHIONS

PILLOWS

BLANKETS OR SHEETS

FRIENDS TO HANG OUT WITH (PEOPLE, STUFFED ANIMALS, DOLLS … ANYONE YOU LIKE!)

Arrange chairs and use the cushions, pillows, and blankets to make a fort-style sukkah right in your own living room. Make it big or small, as long as there is room for friends inside. Practice welcoming your guests by inviting them into the sukkah, making them comfortable, and offering them something to eat or drink. Before you put the pillows away, have a family picnic dinner inside!

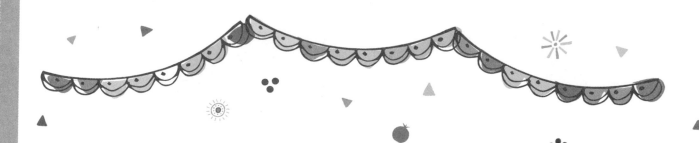

MAKE FRUITY DECORATIONS

Celebrate the fall harvest with beautiful decorations to hang in your sukkah — or anywhere!

CREATE A FRUIT COLLAGE. Cut pictures of fruit out of a magazine and glue them onto poster board.

HANG SMALL FRUITS FROM THE ROOF OF YOUR SUKKAH (OR ANY CEILING).

MAKE FRUIT STAMP ART. Cut pieces of fruit in half, then dip the cut side in nontoxic paint. Stamp the fruit onto a piece of paper, creating a beautiful impressionistic painting.

MAKE DECORATIVE "FRUIT"

Want to create hanging fruit decorations of your own? If you don't have the real thing, create fruit from foil.

SUPPLIES

ALUMINUM FOIL

MASKING TAPE

PAINT AND PAINTBRUSHES

TWIST TIES

STRING

Choose the fruit or vegetable you would like to make. An easy one to start with is an apple. Roll some foil into an apple-sized ball and cover it completely with masking tape. Paint as desired and allow to dry overnight. When it's dry, make a loop with a twist tie and attach it to the top of the apple with tape. Use string to hang your apple in the sukkah or elsewhere. Make more fruits and veggies in the same way, and enjoy your Sukkot "harvest"!

STEW UNDER THE STARS

Eating a delicious meal under the stars in a beautifully decorated sukkah, surrounded by friends and family, is a special experience. Sukkot meals often include dishes with plenty of seasonal vegetables and fruits. One hearty Sukkot dish is a vegetarian stew.

⋯⋯⋯ ◈ ⋯⋯⋯

INGREDIENTS

½ cup olive oil
¾ cup dried pinto beans
¾ cup dried kidney beans
¾ cup dried navy beans
1 large yellow onion, chopped
¼ cup pearl barley
6 potatoes, peeled and quartered
2 tablespoons paprika
5 cloves garlic, crushed
2 tablespoons honey (or brown sugar)
1 tablespoon soy sauce
1 tablespoon salt
½ teaspoon pepper
14.5-ounce can diced tomatoes
Hot water

⋯⋯⋯ ◈ ⋯⋯⋯

DIRECTIONS

Lightly coat the bottom of your slow cooker (or large pot) with olive oil and cover with all of the beans. Add half of the onion. Sprinkle the barley on top. Put in the potatoes, and cover with the remaining onion. In a separate bowl, mix the paprika, garlic, honey, soy sauce, salt, pepper, and the can of tomatoes with its liquid. Cover this mixture with hot water and stir, then pour it into the slow cooker. Add hot water until the ingredients are just covered. Cook on low for at least 12 hours. Then enjoy!

For more recipes, visit pjlibrary.org/sukkot.

CLOSE-UP: LULAV AND ETROG

The lulav is a cluster of plants: a palm branch, two boughs of willow, and three boughs of myrtle. The etrog is a citron fruit — basically an overgrown lemon. Together the lulav and etrog are called **arba minim** (ahr-BAH mee-NEEM), which is Hebrew for "the four species."

The lulav and etrog reconnect us to a time 3,000 years ago when most Jews in Israel lived as farmers, and the rhythm of life was tied to the land. Sukkot comes right at the end of the fall harvest.

One reason for assembling these four plants is that they grow in four different parts of Israel: the desert (**date palm**), mountains (**myrtle**), river (**willow**), and farmlands (**etrog**). Shaking these plants together — a ritual "rain stick" — is a plea for a year of good rainfall, necessary for plentiful crops and nourishing all living things.

The lulav and etrog together also look a little bit like a body: myrtle leaves look like eyes, willow leaves like lips, a palm branch like a spine, and an etrog like a heart. We hope for an abundant and joyful new year with all our body and soul!

SHAKING THE LULAV AND ETROG

When we shake the lulav and etrog (see page 63) in six directions — forward, right, back, left, up, and down — we create a force field surrounding us on all sides. We hope to be surrounded by and protected by our many blessings this year.

> Gently scratch the peel of your etrog to release its pleasant citrus smell. After Sukkot ends, you can make jam from the etrog. See pjlibrary.org/sukkot for a recipe.

HANDS ON!

MAKE YOUR OWN RAIN STICK

If you don't have a lulav and etrog to shake, try shaking this!

SUPPLIES

CRAFT SUPPLIES
(MARKERS, CRAYONS)

PAPER TOWEL TUBE

SCISSORS

PLASTIC WRAP

TAPE

ALUMINUM FOIL

A HANDFUL OF DRIED BEANS, RICE, OR POPCORN KERNELS

Use your craft supplies to decorate the tube. Use scissors to cut a small piece of plastic wrap, and cover one end of the tube with it, attaching it with tape. Loosely scrunch up a piece of foil into a snakelike shape that is almost as long as the tube. Place the foil inside the tube. Add the beans, rice, or popcorn kernels to the tube. Cap the open end of the tube with more plastic wrap and tape. Tilt the tube back and forth and listen to the rain.

SUKKOT

EVENING

HOLIDAY BLESSINGS

At the beginning of Sukkot, you can make the evening meal festive with special rituals and blessings. For lighting the holiday candles and blessing your children, see pages 16 and 17.

Visit pjlibrary.org/grow to hear the blessings.

KIDDUSH

BLESSING OVER WINE OR GRAPE JUICE

בָּרוּךְ אַתָּה יְיָ אֱלֹהֵינוּ מֶלֶךְ הָעוֹלָם בּוֹרֵא פְּרִי הַגָּפֶן.

Baruch ata Adonai, Eloheinu melech ha'olam,
borei peri hagafen.

Dear God, Creator of our world, thank You
for the delicious fruit that grows on vines.

• •

בָּרוּךְ אַתָּה יְיָ אֱלֹהֵינוּ מֶלֶךְ הָעוֹלָם אֲשֶׁר בָּחַר בָּנוּ מִכָּל עָם וְרוֹמְמָנוּ מִכָּל לָשׁוֹן וְקִדְּשָׁנוּ בְּמִצְוֹתָיו.
וַתִּתֶּן לָנוּ יְיָ אֱלֹהֵינוּ בְּאַהֲבָה (שַׁבָּתוֹת לִמְנוּחָה וּ)מוֹעֲדִים לְשִׂמְחָה חַגִּים וּזְמַנִּים לְשָׂשׂוֹן אֶת יוֹם
(הַשַּׁבָּת הַזֶּה וְאֶת יוֹם) חַג הַסֻּכּוֹת הַזֶּה, זְמַן שִׂמְחָתֵנוּ (בְּאַהֲבָה) מִקְרָא קֹדֶשׁ זֵכֶר לִיצִיאַת מִצְרָיִם.
כִּי בָנוּ בָחַרְתָּ וְאוֹתָנוּ קִדַּשְׁתָּ מִכָּל הָעַמִּים (וְשַׁבָּת) וּמוֹעֲדֵי קָדְשֶׁךָ (בְּאַהֲבָה וּבְרָצוֹן) בְּשִׂמְחָה וּבְשָׂשׂוֹן
הִנְחַלְתָּנוּ. בָּרוּךְ אַתָּה יְיָ מְקַדֵּשׁ (הַשַּׁבָּת וְ)יִשְׂרָאֵל וְהַזְּמַנִּים.

Baruch ata Adonai, Eloheinu melech ha'olam, asher bachar banu mikol am,
veromemanu mikol lashon, vekideshanu bemitzvotav. Vatiten lanu Adonai
Eloheinu b'ahava (Shabbatot limenucha u–) moadim lesimcha chagim
uzmanim lesason, et yom (haShabbat hazeh v'et yom) chag haSukkot hazeh,
zman simchateinu (b'ahava) mikra kodesh, zecher liyetzi'at Mitzrayim. Ki vanu
vacharta v'otanu kidashta mikol ha'amim, (v'Shabbat) umoadei kodshecha
(b'ahava uv'ratzon) b'simcha uv'sason hinchaltanu. Baruch ata Adonai,
mekadesh (haShabbat v') Yisra'el vehazmanim.

Dear God, Creator of our world, You have given all the people in the world different
ways of living and believing. Thank You for giving us the gift of being Jewish and
rules and good deeds that help make us better people. On this festival of Sukkot, a
time of great happiness, we remember how You took us out of slavery in the land
of Egypt. Dear God, thank You for giving us this special holiday.

BLESSING FOR SITTING IN THE SUKKAH

בָּרוּךְ אַתָּה יְיָ אֱלֹהֵינוּ מֶלֶךְ הָעוֹלָם אֲשֶׁר קִדְּשָׁנוּ בְּמִצְוֹתָיו וְצִוָּנוּ לֵישֵׁב בַּסֻּכָּה.

Say this blessing for sitting in the sukkah:

Baruch ata Adonai, Eloheinu melech ha'olam, asher kideshanu bemitzvotav vetzivanu leisheiv basukkah.

Dear God, Creator of our world, thank You for this special opportunity to sit in the sukkah.

When eating in the sukkah for the first time this year, also add the following blessing:

בָּרוּךְ אַתָּה יְיָ אֱלֹהֵינוּ מֶלֶךְ הָעוֹלָם שֶׁהֶחֱיָנוּ וְקִיְּמָנוּ וְהִגִּיעָנוּ לַזְּמַן הַזֶּה.

Baruch ata Adonai, Eloheinu melech ha'olam, shehecheyanu vekiyemanu vehigi'anu lazman hazeh.

Dear God, Creator of our world, thank You for keeping us alive so we can celebrate this important moment.

WASHING HANDS & EATING CHALLAH

As on Rosh Hashanah, it is traditional to dip challah in honey for Sukkot. Keep bringing in the sweetness of a new year!

For blessings on washing hands and eating challah, see page 20.

SHAKING THE LULAV AND ETROG

It's customary to shake a lulav and etrog in the sukkah on each morning of Sukkot. But shaking any time of day is fine, especially if you're all gathered together for a festive meal.

Hold the lulav in your right hand and the etrog in your left hand with the tip of the etrog pointing toward the ground. Bring the lulav and etrog together so they're touching and say this blessing:

בָּרוּךְ אַתָּה יְיָ אֱלֹהֵינוּ מֶלֶךְ הָעוֹלָם אֲשֶׁר קִדְּשָׁנוּ בְּמִצְוֹתָיו וְצִוָּנוּ עַל נְטִילַת לוּלָב.

Baruch ata Adonai, Eloheinu melech ha'olam, asher kideshanu bemitzvotav vetzivanu al netilat lulav.

Dear God, Creator of our world, thank You for this opportunity to shake the lulav.

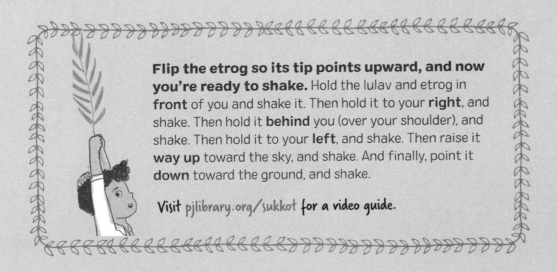

Flip the etrog so its tip points upward, and now you're ready to shake. Hold the lulav and etrog in **front** of you and shake it. Then hold it to your **right**, and shake. Then hold it **behind** you (over your shoulder), and shake. Then hold it to your **left**, and shake. Then raise it **way up** toward the sky, and shake. And finally, point it **down** toward the ground, and shake.

Visit pjlibrary.org/sukkot for a video guide.

SUKKOT ACTIVITIES

★ ★ ★ ★ ★ ★ ★ ★ ★

Sukkot is a time to gather and celebrate. Here are suggested activities your family can do in a sukkah (or in your house) to make this week a "time of joy" — in your family's own unique way.

INVITE REAL GUESTS ...

Sukkot is a wonderful time to host guests or be a guest. What family or friends can you get together with? Is there someone you've never invited over before or someone new to your community or neighborhood? Everyone enjoys eating in a **sukkah** — and everyone enjoys a little holiday hospitality.

★ ★ ★ ★ ★ ★ ★ ★

FAMILY ACTIVITIES

Try making a new dish to serve at home or bring as a guest. For recipe ideas, visit pjlibrary.org/sukkot. Videoconference with relatives or friends who live far away (and maybe you haven't spoken to in a while). Welcome them virtually into your sukkah or to your table to reconnect.

AND IMAGINARY GUESTS

The first "sukkah" in Jewish history was built by Abraham and Sarah, the first Jews. They lived in the wilderness in a tent that was open on all sides to welcome travelers passing by. On Sukkot we return the favor: In a custom called **ushpizin** (Aramaic for "guests"), we invite Abraham and Sarah into our sukkah along with other legendary figures of the Jewish past.

★ ★ ★ ★ ★ ★ ★ ★

FAMILY ACTIVITIES

Go around the table discussing this question: If you could invite anyone from the past or the present (or even from a book or movie) as a guest for a meal in a sukkah, who would you invite? Why them? For extra fun, dress up as a surprise guest and show up at your own table. Have someone interview you!

SONGS, TOASTS & MORE

In ancient Israel, people made a pilgrimage to Jerusalem during Sukkot, coming from near and far to bring part of their harvest to the Temple. On the streets, people would juggle flaming torches, do handstands, play instruments, and dance and sing, causing the rabbis to say, "If you haven't seen this celebration, you've never experienced true joy." Sukkot is a special opportunity for your family to party together!

★ ★ ★ ★ ★ ★ ★ ★

FAMILY ACTIVITIES

Prepare song sheets so everyone has the lyrics. Pass them around and start singing! Make a playlist with your favorite dance songs (visit pjlibrary.org/grow for some ready-to-go dance mixes) and shake your body like a lulav and etrog! Make toasts on grape juice ("**L'chaim**! To life!"). Or go mellow: Have a game night or a candlelit story hour. Read a PJ Library book while cuddling in the sukkah (a couch works too).

STARGAZING AND SLEEPOVERS

A sukkah's roof lets us see the night sky with a full moon and stars. (Stars helped the Israelites navigate their journey through the desert wilderness.) Any evening that's not too cloudy or wet could be a good night for stargazing.

The last day of Sukkot has a special name: **Hoshana Rabbah** (basically, Hebrew for "help is on the way"). In ancient times, people would march around the Temple in Jerusalem holding the lulav and etrog, wishing for rain and good things in the year ahead. It also became customary to stay up through the night learning together. Then on the following morning — in a dramatic finale — it's traditional to hit willow boughs from the lulav against the ground until all the leaves fall off, symbolizing a final farewell to our bad actions from the past year.

★ ★ ★ ★ ★ ★ ★ ★

FAMILY ACTIVITIES

Pick a night for stargazing with family or friends. Combine it with a final-night sleepover, in a sukkah or in the house. In the morning, take the willow boughs from your lulav (if you have one) and hit them against the ground!

SIMCHAT TORAH

CELEBRATING THE TREE OF LIFE

The Jewish New Year season ends with one last celebration: **Simchat Torah** (seem-CHAHT toe-RAH) — "Rejoicing with the Torah." Torah means "teaching" in Hebrew. The word is used to describe the first five books of the Bible that tell the story of the Jewish people.

The Torah story is read over the course of an entire year. On Simchat Torah, we finish reading the very last part of the Torah scroll and then roll it all the way back to read the beginning.

On this holiday we even dance with the Torah because its words are so important to us. The Torah is sometimes described as a "tree of life for those who take care of it" — like a tree giving people what they need to grow. Throughout the year, studying the Torah can provide us with new inspiration and ideas.

Each year, the Torah's stories will challenge you in new ways. How can they help you grow?

APPRECIATING RAIN

Look outside the window. If it's raining, reflect on how much your life depends on water.

"Whenever the rainbow appears in the clouds, it will be a reminder of the partnership between God and all living creatures." Genesis 9:16

Restarting the Torah comes at the beginning of the rainy season in Israel. On the day before Simchat Torah (or on the holiday itself) is a celebration called **Shemini Atzeret** (she-MEE-nee ah-TZEHR-eht). On this day it's traditional to say a special blessing for rain to remind ourselves how all growing things depend on water.

Mizrahi (Middle Eastern) Jews say a special prayer that describes different kinds of rain:

With rains of light, brighten the earth.
With rains of blessing, bless the land.
With joyful rains, fertilize the soil.
With singing rains, make the ground sing.
With rains of life, bring life to the land.
With rains of goodness, help reclaim the earth.

FAMILY DISCUSSION

What words would you use to describe different kinds of rain? Think about warm summer rains soaking your hair, the sound of an autumn thunderstorm (a little scary?), or the fun of splashing in puddles anytime!

CANDY-APPLE MAKING

You can enjoy a delicious holiday custom: candy-apple making. Eating candy apples on Simchat Torah is a tradition for celebrating the sweet "tree of life." Try making this easy recipe together as a family.

8 small apples
4 full-size chocolate bars (milk or dark)
8 small wooden forks or craft sticks
Colored or chocolate sprinkles
Nuts (optional)
Parchment paper

Wash and dry the apples. Break the chocolate into pieces and melt it using the stovetop or microwave (a grown-up's job). Stick a wooden fork in the top of each apple. One at a time, dip each apple into the melted chocolate and let the excess drip off. Roll the apple in sprinkles and/or nuts and put it on parchment paper. Place the dipped apples in the refrigerator until the coating hardens.

CRAFTING A TORAH

Jewish people have been making Torah scrolls for thousands of years, carefully copying the same words generation after generation. There are 304,805 Hebrew letters in the Torah, so it can take an entire year to produce a Torah scroll.

First, the parchment needs to be prepared. Then special ink is made with unusual ingredients, including tree sap and pomegranate peels. Each letter is carefully written with a pen made from a feather. The finished scroll is wrapped around wooden poles and then covered with a cloth or a case. Some scrolls also have a silver crown placed on top.

FAMILY ACTIVITY

The Torah scrolls in synagogues are very expensive and time-consuming to make. But you can make your own scroll to celebrate with at home from simple materials around the house.

1. Decorate a **brown paper lunch bag** with pictures, stickers, and designs for Simchat Torah.
2. Cover **two paper towel tubes** with **aluminum foil.** These will be the two "poles."
3. Cut holes in the bottom of the bag so the paper towel tubes can stick out the top and bottom of the bag.
4. Glue or tape each tube to the bag.

Your Torah toy can even be used as a bag to carry stickers, games, and activities to synagogue, or to dance with at home to celebrate Simchat Torah!

SIMCHAT TORAH
EVENING

DANCING WITH THE TORAH

On the evening when Simchat Torah begins, communities around the world celebrate with dancing, singing, and even special sweet treats for children. The party is one last chance to express gratitude for the amazing gift of the Torah.

People carry Torah scrolls in a procession around the synagogue while singing joyful songs. Parents hoist kids up on their shoulders, children wave homemade flags, and everyone celebrates. In some communities, roads are blocked off so people can dance with Torah scrolls in the streets.

FAMILY ACTIVITY

You can also dance at home! Kids can celebrate while hugging stuffed animals, lifting up their homemade Torah scrolls, waving flags, and enjoying treats. Visit **pjlibrary.org/grow** for a Simchat Torah dance playlist.

SIMCHAT TORAH
DAY

NEVER-ENDING STORY

It is a tradition on Simchat Torah morning to read the last sentences of the Torah, and then to wind the scroll all the way back to the beginning to read the Torah's first sentences. Here is a modern retelling of both sections.

" " " " " " " " " "

The end of the Torah:

After the Israelites escaped from slavery in Egypt, Moses led them through the desert for 40 years. At last, they were about to enter the Land of Israel. Now an old man, Moses stood on a mountaintop looking across at the land of his ancestors, but he would not cross the Jordan River into Israel.

" " " " " " " " " "

Now rewind to the start of the Torah:

In the beginning, God began to create the sky and the earth. God said: "Let there be light" — and there was light. God saw that the light was good and separated light from darkness. God called the light "Day" and the darkness "Night." After evening and then morning, the first day ended ...

FAMILY ACTIVITY

Take a book you have enjoyed reading many times. Instead of reading the book from front to back, open the book to the end and read the last page. Then flip all the way to the beginning and read the first page.

THE END OF THE BEGINNING

As Simchat Torah ends, we can look back on our three-week holiday journey.

We have watched the moon grow from a tiny sliver to a giant circle in the night sky and then start to shrink again. Like the moon, we too have taken this time as an opportunity to grow and change and make ourselves new.

We have looked back at the past year to take responsibility for our actions. We have made decisions about how to improve going forward. We have taken steps to make our family and friendships stronger. We have celebrated the wonderful things in our lives that can help us on our journey ahead.

Right after we blow the shofar to end Yom Kippur, we call out **"Next year in Jerusalem!"** — the very same words we say in the spring to end our Passover seder (ritual meal). Our goal is to come to Rosh Hashanah next year as better people and to help the world grow in peace, justice, and well-being.

73

EPILOGUE

ON FARMING & GARDENING

What ties together the holidays of this
season, beginning with Rosh Hashanah
and culminating in Simchat Torah?

Historically, one might point to
farming. Most Jews in ancient
Israel were farmers. At this time of
year, they rushed to harvest their produce
and plant new crops before the rains

began. They sowed seeds — the seeds of a
new growing year — and planted damaged
wheat kernels in the ground (*kippur*, as in
Yom Kippur, originally meant to cover a
seed with dirt, turning something flawed

into an opportunity for growth). After weeks of intense work, they joyfully celebrated the fruits of their labor. In this way, the rhythm of ancient farming may have served as a template for this holiday season.

Everything ultimately came down to one thing: rain. While all other civilizations of the region were sustained by vast rivers, ancient Israel was dependent on rainfall. The Israelites turned their gaze to the heavens. And when, after a long dry spring and summer, a downpour finally came, the world was revitalized. In Hebrew, the word for that first miraculous rain — *yoreh* — comes from the same root as *Torah*, "learning." Just as first rains created channels of flowing water across the land, the Torah creates paths that nourish and navigate Jewish life. **Even if we aren't farmers, we are — in a real sense — all gardeners, and the most important thing we're growing is our children.** Each time the Jewish New Year comes around, we want to improve as people, in part, because our children are learning from us how to be in the world. We also learn from <u>them</u> that the world is an ever-widening and ever-changing place, full of wonder and possibility.

It's impossible not to acknowledge our imperfections as parents, but each year we recommit ourselves to the sacred task at hand — of giving our children the best possible conditions to grow in, to become whoever they will become. If the High Holidays focus on who we — and our children — might still become, then Sukkot and Simchat Torah let us revel in what is: the beauty of nature, the joy of family and community, and the wisdom of our tradition.

In raising children, writes PJ Library author Laurel Snyder, we "plant another kind of seed ... People are gardens too, and they bear the fruit tended by many generations of gardeners."

For additional resources,
visit **pjlibrary.org/grow**.

FAMILY CONVERSATIONS

The Ten Days (including Rosh Hashanah and Yom Kippur) are a good time for having thoughtful one-on-one conversations or a sit-down talk as a whole family. You can use these prompts to guide you. **Want to learn more? See page 35.**

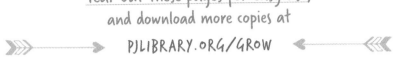

Tear out these pages for easy use,
and download more copies at
PJLIBRARY.ORG/GROW

1

THINK ABOUT YOUR ACTIONS.

MAKING MYSELF (EVEN) BETTER

What things have I done this past year that I'm proud of?

_____

_____

What can I do this new year that I'll be proud of?

_____

_____

How can I get started?

_____

_____

2

HAVE A ONE-ON-ONE CONVERSATION WITH A FAMILY MEMBER OR FRIEND.

MAKING FAMILY AND FRIENDSHIPS STRONGER

What are some kind things we've done for each other this past year?

_____

_____

How have we disrespected or hurt each other this past year? Now is the time to apologize for those acts and to offer each other forgiveness.

_____

_____

What's the best way to keep these things from happening again?

_____

_____

3

FAMILY GOALS

SIT AS A FAMILY
TO DISCUSS YOUR
GOALS FOR THE
NEW YEAR AND
WAYS TO GROW
EVEN KINDER TO
EACH OTHER.

When do we feel most connected as a family? When is it harder to get along?

_____

_____

How can we support each other better?

_____

_____

What are some ideas for making family time more special in the new year?

_____

_____

_____

_____

=== EXAMPLES ===

No phones or gossip (lashon hara) at the
dinner table. Sharing Friday night (Shabbat)
dinner together. Eating healthier food
or spending more time outdoors together. ↘

4

AS A FAMILY,
DISCUSS WAYS
TO REACH OUT TO
OTHERS IN YOUR
NEIGHBORHOOD,
YOUR COMMUNITY,
AND THE WORLD.

FIXING THE WORLD (tikkun olam in Hebrew)

Do we have a neighbor who lives alone or friends who are going through a difficult time? What can we do to help them?

_____

_____

Are there people in our community who need food, clothes, or shelter? Are there people who aren't treated fairly? What are some ways we can support them?

_____

_____

What are our tikkun olam goals (helping animals, helping the environment, visiting the elderly, etc.) and what project ideas can we think up?

_____

_____

_____

═══ TIP ═══

If your family has a tzedakah box for collecting money for charitable donations, this is a good time of year to talk about where to give the money when the box gets full.